Questions and Answers: Countries

Cuba

A Question and Answer Book

by Muriel L. Dubois

Consultant:
Sandra Levinson, President
Center for Cuban Studies
New York City, New York

Capstone
press

Mankato, Minnesota

Fact Finders is published by Capstone Press,
151 Good Counsel Drive, P.O. Box 669, Mankato, Minnesota 56002.
www.capstonepress.com

Library of Congress Cataloging-in-Publication Data
Dubois, Muriel L.
   Cuba: a question and answer book / by Muriel L. Dubois.
   p. cm.—(Fact finders. Questions and answers. Countries)
   Includes bibliographical references and index.
   ISBN 0-7368-3749-3 (hardcover)
   1. Cuba—Juvenile literature. I. Title. II. Series.
F1758.5.D83 2005
972.91—dc22   2004009807

Summary: Describes the geography, history, economy, and culture of Cuba in a
   question-and-answer format.

Editorial Credits
Donald Lemke, editor; Kia Adams, set designer; Kate Opseth, book designer; Nancy Steers,
   map illustrator; Wanda Winch, photo researcher; Scott Thoms, photo editor

Photo Credits
Art Directors/Keith Cardwell, 18–19; Art Directors/M Barlow, 25; Art Directors/Tibor
Bognar, cover (background); Bruce Coleman Inc./Mark Newman, 12–13; Capstone Press,
29 (coins); Corbis/Bettmann, 7, 9; Corbis/Les Stone, 23; Houserstock/Dave G. Houser,
cover (foreground), 1, 8, 11; Houserstock/Jan Butchofsky, 15; Photo courtesy of Richard
Sutherland, 29 (bill); South American Pictures/Rolando Pujol, 21, 27; South American
Pictures/Tony Morrison, 16–17; StockHaus Ltd., 29 (flag); SuperStock/Angelo Cavalli, 4

Artistic Effects
Comstock, 16; Ingram Publishing, 12, 20; Photodisc/Jules Frazier, 18; Photodisc/Siede Preis, 6

1 2 3 4 5 6 10 09 08 07 06 05

Table of Contents

Features

Where is Cuba?

Cuba is a country of many islands. These islands help divide the Atlantic Ocean from the Caribbean Sea. Cuba is also the name of the country's largest island. This island is slightly smaller than the U.S. state of Pennsylvania.

The city of Santiago de Cuba is located at the foot of the Sierra Maestra. ➤

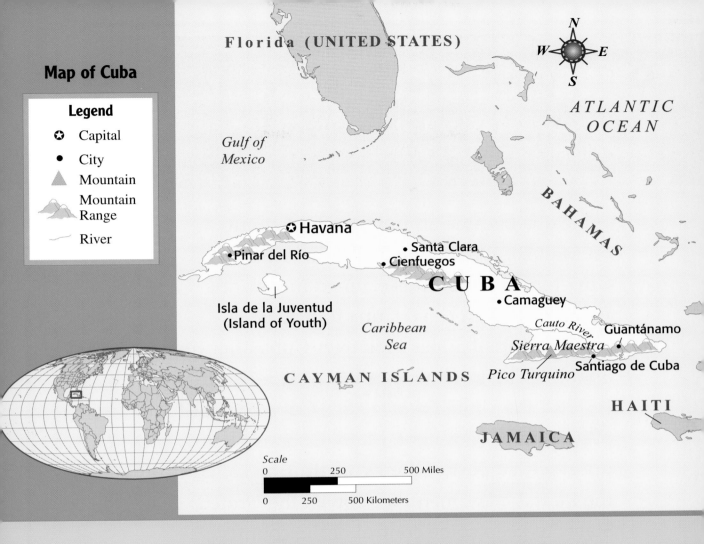

Map of Cuba

Legend
- ✪ Capital
- ● City
- ▲ Mountain
- ⛰ Mountain Range
- ～ River

Florida (UNITED STATES)

Gulf of Mexico

ATLANTIC OCEAN

BAHAMAS

✪ Havana
● Pinar del Río
● Santa Clara
● Cienfuegos

CUBA

● Camaguey

Isla de la Juventud (Island of Youth)

Caribbean Sea

Cauto River

Sierra Maestra

Guantánamo ●

Pico Turquino

Santiago de Cuba

CAYMAN ISLANDS

HAITI

JAMAICA

Scale
0 ... 250 ... 500 Miles
0 ... 250 ... 500 Kilometers

Mountains cover part of the island of Cuba. Pico Turquino is the country's tallest peak. It is located in the Sierra Maestra.

Cuba has more than 2,000 miles (3,200 kilometers) of coastline. Hundreds of sandy beaches cover the coast.

When did Cuba become a country?

Cuba became an **independent** country on May 20, 1902. About 400 years earlier, Christopher Columbus claimed the islands for Spain. Spain ruled Cuba until 1898.

The United States took over Cuba after the Spanish-Cuban-American War (1895–1898). In 1902, the United States gave Cuba control of its own government. Many Cubans were upset with a part of their **constitution** called the Platt Amendment. It allowed the United States to keep some control of the country.

Fact!

Christopher Columbus described Cuba as the most beautiful land ever seen by human eyes.

As Cuba's leader, Fulgencio Batista gave emotional speeches to the people of Cuba.

Several Cuban leaders wanted to free the country from any U.S. control. In 1933, Fulgencio Batista and his army took power. During Batista's rule, Cuba signed a treaty with the United States. It put an end to official U.S. control of Cuba's government.

What type of government does Cuba have?

Cuba is a **socialist** country ruled by a **communist party**. The government owns most of the land, houses, and businesses.

Cubans elect 589 party members to the National Assembly of People's Power. This assembly meets twice a year. They make the country's laws and choose members for the Council of State.

The National Capitol in Havana is where Cuba's government workers meet. ▶

Fidel Castro (center) and members of his revolutionary army overthrew President Batista and took control of Cuba in 1959.

The Council of State runs Cuba when the assembly is not meeting. Council members include the president and first vice president.

On January 1, 1959, Fidel Castro became Cuba's leader. As president, Castro chooses a Council of Ministers to help make laws.

What kind of housing does Cuba have?

Cuba's government promises housing for every family. Many times, builders cannot keep up with the need for homes. In cities, several families often share a house or an apartment.

Cubans must get government permission to buy or sell their houses. Sometimes, families trade houses with each other.

Where do people in Cuba live?

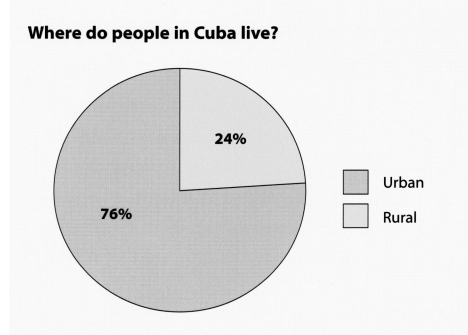

24%

76%

Urban

Rural

In Havana and other cities, many Cubans live in run-down apartment buildings.

In areas outside cities, some Cubans still live in *bohios*. These small houses are made of mud or wood. They often have dirt floors and roofs made of palm leaves. Cuba's government builds apartments to help people move out of *bohios*.

11

What are Cuba's forms of transportation?

Travel within Cuba is difficult. Few people own cars. Most cars in the country are old and need repair. New parts are expensive and hard to find. The Cuban government also **rations** the amount of gas people can buy. It wants everyone to have an equal share of the country's supply.

Instead of driving, many people pedal bikes or walk to work. In cities, some Cubans use their bikes as taxis. They pull people across town in small carts.

Fact!

Camellos *is Spanish for camels. Many people think these long buses look like the humpbacked animals.*

Long buses called camellos *often carry about 250 people around Cuban cities.*

Cubans also travel on trains and buses. In the capital city of Havana, people ride buses known as *guaguas*. They also squeeze onto long buses called *camellos*. Trains run from Havana to Santiago de Cuba and other cities.

What are Cuba's major industries?

Tourism is important to Cuba's **economy**. Many Cubans support their families with jobs at popular tourist spots. They work at hotels, shops, and restaurants.

Cubans also farm and fish. Farmers grow sugarcane and tobacco. They also grow bananas, potatoes, and rice. Cuban fishers catch lobster, red snapper, and shrimp off the country's coasts.

What does Cuba import and export?	
Imports	**Exports**
food	nickel
machinery and equipment	sugar
petroleum	tobacco

Many farmers in Cuba grow tobacco. The country is known around the world for its tobacco products.

Mining and **manufacturing** are also important. Cubans mine nickel and copper. Factories make steel, chemicals, and medicine.

Cubans ship goods to many countries. Since 1961, the U.S. government has refused to do business with Cuba. Its leaders disagree with Cuba's leaders.

What is school like in Cuba?

Children in Cuba begin their education when they are 6 years old. They attend six years of grade school. They then spend three years in basic secondary school. Students study many subjects, including math, science, and reading. Secondary school students also learn about farming and other outdoor work. The Cuban government wants everyone to respect all types of work.

Fact!

In Cuba, all public schools and colleges are free.

In Cuba, some grade school students share desks.

After secondary school, some students go to upper secondary school. These students take classes to prepare for college. Other students go to technical secondary schools. They learn job skills.

What are Cuba's favorite sports and games?

Baseball is the national sport of Cuba. Many Cubans play on fields or even in the streets. Cuba does not have any pro teams. The best players often compete in the United States. Others play on Cuba's national team.

Cubans enjoy many other sports and games. Soccer and volleyball are popular with children and adults. One of the most common games is dominoes. Every year, the best players compete in the World Championship of Dominoes.

Fact!

Cuba's national baseball team won gold medals at the 1992, 1996, and 2004 Olympic Games.

Children in Cuba often play baseball in the street with friends.

From age 11 to 16, Cubans compete in the School Sports Games. Winners get to try out for special schools for sports. Students at these schools get extra coaching. Many of them become Olympic athletes.

What are the traditional art forms in Cuba?

Music is an important part of Cuban life. *Son* is a popular style of Cuban music. It mixes African drumbeats with Spanish singing. *Son* musicians play guitars, drums, maracas, and other instruments. Many people enjoy *son* music around the world.

Most Cuban towns have a house of song. People come to these small buildings to play or listen to music.

Fact!

The habanera, cha-cha, and mambo sound like the names of spicy foods. They are actually Cuban dances.

People in Cuba enjoy dancing and playing music.

Cubans also enjoy telling stories. Cuban stories from Africa are called *patakines*. People in Cuba have shared these religious tales for hundreds of years. Many of them were never written down. *Patakin* storytellers often use drums to help tell their stories.

What major holidays do people in Cuba celebrate?

Cubans celebrate national holidays that honor their government. On July 26, 1953, Fidel Castro and his supporters attacked Fort Moncada in Santiago de Cuba. Rebellion Day honors this attack as the start of a struggle against Batista's rule. On January 1, 1959, Castro and his supporters took control of the government. Cubans celebrate this day as Liberation Day.

What other holidays do people in Cuba celebrate?

Christmas
Commencement of the Wars of Independence
Days of the Rebel Conquest
Labor Day

Every year, people celebrate the anniversary of Cuba's revolution.

Cubans often combine religious festivals. In December, they honor the Catholic Saint Lazarus and the African god Babalú Ayé. In the Cuban religion of Santería, these religious figures are the same saint. People visit a church in Havana that honors both of them.

What are the traditional foods of Cuba?

Cubans eat basic foods, such as chicken, rice, and beans. One common dish is made with black beans and rice. Cubans call this dish Moors and Christians.

The Cuban government rations the country's food supply. It wants families to have enough food to stay healthy. Still, some Cubans do not get enough to eat.

Fact!

Cubans drink sugarcane juice called guarapo. Surprisingly, this pure sugar juice is only as sweet as most soft drinks.

In Havana, people buy sweet potatoes and other vegetables at local markets.

Cubans often eat foods from local farmers and fishers. Plantains and sweet potatoes are served at many meals. Seafood and fish are also common. Grouper, red snapper, and lobster are Cuban favorites.

What is family life like in Cuba?

Cuba is the only country with a law describing the duties of each family member. In 1975, Cuba's government passed the Family Code. This law says that both parents must help support their children. They must also share work around the house.

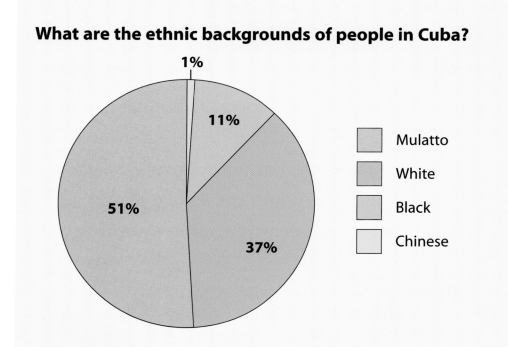

What are the ethnic backgrounds of people in Cuba?

1%

11%

51%

37%

Mulatto

White

Black

Chinese

Families in Cuba enjoy spending time together.

The Family Code encouraged more Cuban women to get jobs. Today, both parents often work outside the home. Children stay at day care or with family and friends.

Cubans still find time for family. They often eat a meal together in the evening.

Cuba Fast Facts

Official name:

Republic of Cuba

Population:

11,308,764 people

Land area:

*42,803 square miles
(110,860 square kilometers)*

Capital city:

Havana

**Average annual
precipitation:**

52 inches (132 centimeters)

Language:

Spanish

**Average January
temperature:**

*73 degrees Fahrenheit
(23 degrees Celsius)*

Natural resources:

*cobalt, copper, farmland, iron ore,
manganese, nickel, petroleum,
salt, silica, timber*

**Average July
temperature:**

*82 degrees Fahrenheit
(28 degrees Celsius)*

Religions:

*Santería and/or Catholic   70%
Nonreligious   30%*

Money and Flag

Money:

Cuba's money is called the peso. In 2004, 1 U.S. dollar equaled 21 Cuban pesos. One Canadian dollar equaled 15.34 Cuban pesos.

Flag:

Cuba's flag has three blue stripes and two white stripes. The blue stripes stand for the three parts of government. The white stripes mean purity. The red triangle reminds Cubans of their fight for independence. The white star stands for freedom.

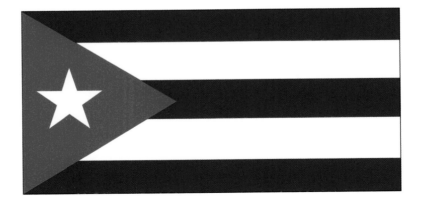

Learn to Speak Spanish

People in Cuba speak Spanish. It is Cuba's official language. Learn to speak some Spanish words using the chart below.

English	Spanish	Pronunciation
hello	hola	(OH-lah)
good morning	buenos días	(BWAY-nohs DEE-ahs)
good-bye	adiós	(ah-dee-OHS)
please	por favor	(POR fah-VOR)
thank you	gracias	(GRAH-see-us)
yes	sí	(SEE)
no	no	(NOH)
boy	niño	(NEEN-yoh)
girl	niña	(NEEN-yah)

Glossary

communist party (KOM-yuh-nihst PAR-tee)—a political party that believes all land, houses, and businesses should belong to the government

constitution (kon-stuh-TOO-shuhn)—the written system of laws in a country that states the rights of the people and the powers of government

economy (i-KON-uh-mee)—the way a country runs its industry, trade, and finance

independent (in-di-PEN-duhnt)—free from the control of other people or things

manufacturing (man-yuh-FAK-chur-ing)—the process of making something

ration (RASH-uhn)—to give out in limited amounts

socialist (SOH-shuh-lihst)—an economic system in which the goods made by factories, businesses, and farms are controlled by the government

tourism (TOOR-iz-um)—the business of providing entertainment, food, and lodging for travelers

Internet Sites

FactHound offers a safe, fun way to find Internet sites related to this book. All of the sites on FactHound have been researched by our staff.

Here's how:
1. Visit *www.facthound.com*
2. Type in this special code **0736837493** for age-appropriate sites. Or enter a search word related to this book for a more general search.
3. Click on the **Fetch It** button.

FactHound will fetch the best sites for you!

Read More

Britton, Tamara L. *Cuba.* The Countries. Edina, Minn.: Abdo, 2002.

Doak, Robin S. *Cuba.* First Reports. Minneapolis: Compass Point Books, 2004.

Gordon, Sharon. *Cuba.* Discovering Cultures. Tarrytown, N.Y.: Benchmark Books, 2003.

Stevens, Kathryn. *Cuba.* Faces and Places. Chanhassen, Minn.: Child's World, 2002.

Index